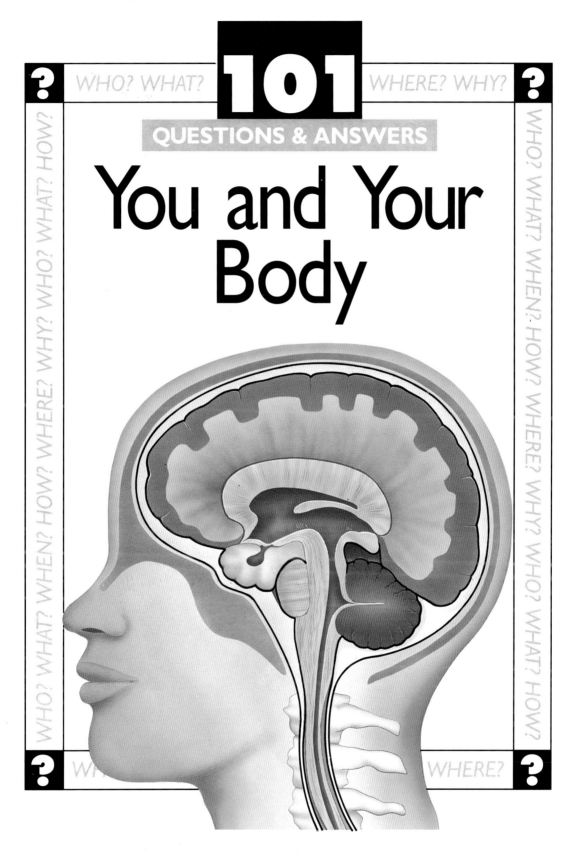

101

QUESTIONS & ANSWERS

You and Your Body

Facts On File®

AN INFOBASE HOLDINGS COMPANY

GLOSSARY

bacteria Tiny specks of life, no larger than a cell. Most bacteria are harmless to the body, but some cause disease.

calcium A mineral that helps to make teeth and bones hard. Milk, cheese and eggs contain calcium.

carbohydrate Foods, such as sugar, bread, pasta, rice and potatoes, from which the body gets energy.

carbon dioxide A waste gas breathed out with air from the lungs.

cartilage Rubbery gristle that protects the ends of bones in a joint.

cell Smallest living unit. The human body is made up of millions of cells.

chromosome Each chromosome contains hundreds of genes that determine our sex and how we look. Each body cell has the same chromosomes; half were inherited from the mother, half from the father.

digestion The process of breaking down food into separate particles, small enough to be absorbed into the blood.

enzymes Chemicals produced by the body to help break down food in the digestive system.

evaporation The process by which liquid changes into a vapor.

fertilize An egg cell is fertilized when it combines with a sperm and so can grow into a new life.

fiber Long, thin thread. Muscles and nerves are made of different kinds of fiber.

gene A list of coded instructions that dictate all our physical characteristics. Most features are determined by several genes.

gland Some glands produce hormones that are released into the blood. Other glands, such as sweat and salivary glands, release special substances just where they are.

hormone Chemical produced by some glands to control particular processes in the body. For example, the pituitary hormone controls growth.

intestines Long tube that joins the stomach to the rectum and through which most food is digested.

joint Where two bones meet. Most joints allow one bone to move separately from the other.

marrow Jelly-like substance at the center of some bones, which manufactures blood cells.

molecule The smallest particle of a substance that can exist on its own.

mucus A clear liquid that protects tubes inside the body.

nerve Fiber that carries electrical messages to or from the brain.

organ A part of the body, such as the liver, that does a particular job.

oxygen Gas needed by all living things. Humans breathe in oxygen from the air.

protein Special food that cells need to renew and maintain themselves. Fish, meat, eggs, cheese and beans all contain protein.

puberty Time when the body changes from a child's to an adult's capable of having children.

senses Sight, hearing, smell, taste and touch are the means by which the brain receives information from the outside world.

spinal cord Collection of nerves that run through and are protected by the vertebrae of the spine.

tendon Bundle of fibers that attach a muscle to a bone.

tissue Living matter made up of just one kind of cell.

vitamin Special foods that the body needs to work well.

The 101 Questions and Answers series contains six titles that cover a range of scientific topics popular with young readers, such as: the human body, geology, basic mechanics and physics, dinosaurs, and transportation. Each book is designed in a question-and-answer format with color illustrations throughout.

You and Your Body

Facts On File books are available at special discounts when purchased in bulk quantities for businesses, associations, institutions or sales promotions. Please call our Special Sales Department in New York at 212/683-2244 or 800/322-8755.

10 9 8 7 6 5 4 3 2 1

This book is printed on acid-free paper.

Printed in Italy

Library of Congress Cataloging-in-Publication Data
Royston, Angela.
    You and your body / [Angela Royston]
      p. cm. -- (101 questions & answers)
    Includes index.
    ISBN 0-8160-3217-3
    1. Body, Human--Juvenile literature. 2. Human anatomy--Juvenile literature. [1. Body, Human--Miscellanea. 2. Human physiology--Miscellanea. 3. Questions and answers.] I. Title. II. Series.
    QM27.R69 1995
    612--dc20   95-16304

Acknowledgments
Designer: Ben White
Project Editor: Lionel Bender
Text Editor: Madeleine Samuel
Media Conversion and Typesetting: Peter MacDonald and Una Macnamara
Managing Editor: David Riley
Production Controller: Ruth Charlton
Artwork: pages 4, 5c, 6t, 7t, 9cl, 18, 25, 26-27, 28, 29, 34, 35, 36l, 38, 39, 40, 41 by Peter Bull Art Studio; 5b, 47b (inset) by Bill Prosser; 6b, 7b, 26b, 36r, 37 by Tony Randell; 8, 9bl, 9c, 10-11, 14-15, 32-33 by Frank Kennard; 12-13, 16-17, 19, 30-31, 42, 43, 45 by John Bovosier; 27b, 44b, 46b, 46-47 Darren Patterson. (t = top, b = bottom, l = left, r = right, c = center).

CONTENTS

This book contains questions and answers on the following topics:

Angela Royston

How thick is my skin?

Most of your skin is just 0.8 in (2 mm) thick. Skin consists of two main layers – the epidermis and the dermis. The surface of the skin is covered with hard, tough dead cells that flake off all the time. They are replaced by cells from the epidermis below.

Skin protects your body from the outside world. It stops dirt, germs and radiation from the sun getting in, and it stops your body losing moisture and drying out. The fine hairs on your skin help to keep you warm, but skin also stops you getting too hot. Sweat glands pump out tiny drops of water that evaporate to cool your skin.

DID YOU KNOW...
● The thickest skin (about 0.6 in, or 3 mm) is on the soles of the feet?
● You have about 3 million sweat glands all over your body?
● Women have the same number of body hairs as men? They are just less noticeable.

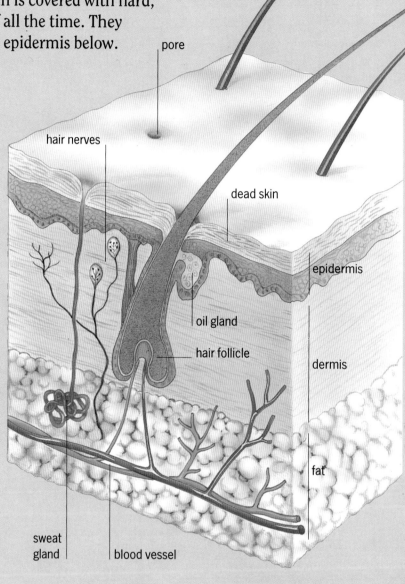

pore
hair nerves
dead skin
epidermis
oil gland
hair follicle
dermis
fat
sweat gland
blood vessel

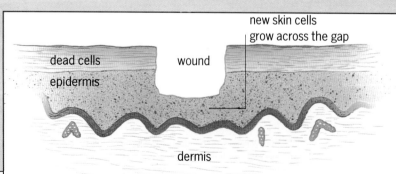

new skin cells grow across the gap
wound
dead cells
epidermis
dermis

HOW DO CUTS HEAL?
Blood and skin work together to heal a wound. Blood fills the gap and thickens to form a clot, which slowly dries into a hard scab. New skin grows underneath. You can see it when the scab falls off. It is pinker than old skin.

Why does skin tan?

Your skin contains a special substance called melanin. It protects you from harmful, ultra-violet radiation in the sun's rays. It also gives your skin its color. Brown skin has more melanin than white skin. If you are in stronger sunshine than usual, your skin produces more melanin and becomes tan.

▶ Melanin is produced by special cells in your skin called melanocytes. The tiny granules of melanin spread throughout the epidermis.

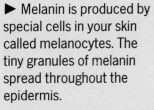

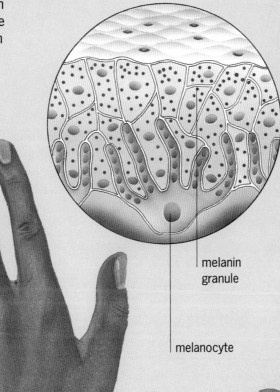

melanin granule

melanocyte

WHY USE SUNTAN LOTION?

Suntan lotion screens out harmful radiation from the sun – just like melanin. It is useful because your skin needs time to make more melanin and extra help to stop you burning. Sunburn can lead to skin cancer.

WHAT ARE FRECKLES AND MOLES?

Freckles are tiny patches of skin that have extra melanin. They tend to fade in winter and reappear in summer. Moles are similar to freckles, but they contain more melanin and do not fade in winter. People with many freckles tend to get sunburned easily.

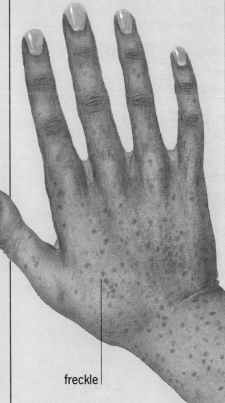

freckle

DARK OR FAIR?

● Melanin gives your hair its color. The more melanin you have the darker it will be.
● People who have no melanin are called albinos. They have white hair and particularly pink skin and eyes.

● Brown-skinned people get darker in the sun too.
● Moles used to be called beauty spots. Fashionable people used to paint false moles on their faces to look more attractive.

Straight hair or curly hair?

How straight, wavy or curly your hair is depends on the shape of the hair follicles in your scalp. Curly hair grows from flat follicles, wavy hair from oval follicles and straight hair from round follicles.

Most people have about 100,000 hairs on their head. They each grow from a follicle buried in tiny mounds in the lower layer of skin. The hair that you see consists of dead cells. It is kept smooth and supple by oil from the oil gland.

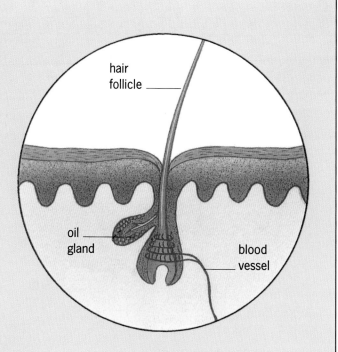

hair follicle

oil gland

blood vessel

CURLY HAIR

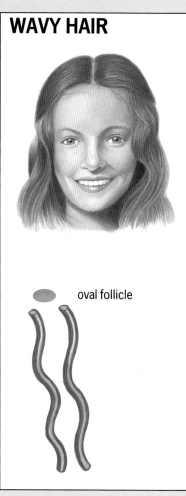

flat follicle

WAVY HAIR

oval follicle

STRAIGHT HAIR

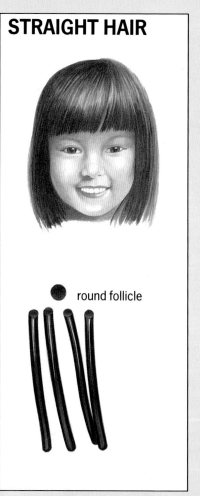

round follicle

How fast do finger and toe nails grow?

Nails grow about .12 in (3 mm) every month, or 1.4 in (3.5 cm) a year. The ends tend to crack and break so, even if you did not cut them, your nails would not grow very long. New nail is formed at the bottom under the skin. It pushes up the older nail. The nail that you see is made of tough, dead cells, so it does not hurt when you cut it. Nails and hair are made of the same substance – keratin. With nails it forms a horny plate at the end of each finger and toe.

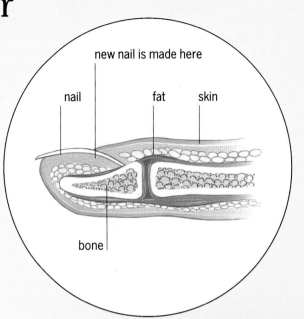

new nail is made here

nail   fat   skin

bone

WHAT ARE NAILS FOR?

Nails protect the ends of the fingers – one of the most sensitive parts of the body. Nails give the flesh and bone something to push against and allow you to make small and difficult movements, like threading a needle, more accurately. If you cut your finger nails very short, you will see how much harder it is to pick up small items.

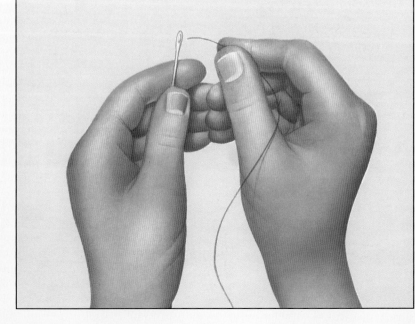

DID YOU KNOW...

● Some people have grown their finger nails several inches long? A monk in India has grown his more than a foot long!

● Nails and hair are made of the same substance as animal horns and claws?

● The hair on your head grows about 0.1 in (0.33 mm) every day? That is about 4.8 in (12 cm) every year or 28 ft (8.5 m) in a lifetime.

● Every day you lose between 30 and 60 hairs? After a while the hair follicle withers and the hair falls out. The follicle rests for 3 or 4 months before a new hair starts to grow.

● Since each hair lasts only about 6 years, most people cannot grow their hair longer than about 3.3 ft (1 m)?

● Men start to go bald when their hair follicles stop producing new hair? Many cures have been tried but none found!

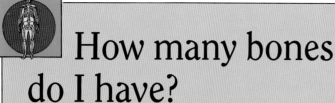

How many bones do I have?

As a baby you had more than 350 bones, but as you grow some of them join together. By the time you are adult you will have about 208. Nearly half of all your bones are in your hands, wrists, feet and ankles. The biggest bone is the thigh bone or femur and the smallest is the stirrup, a bone in each of your ears.

Bones support you, give your body its shape and protect your insides from injury. Your ribs, for example, protect your heart and lungs.

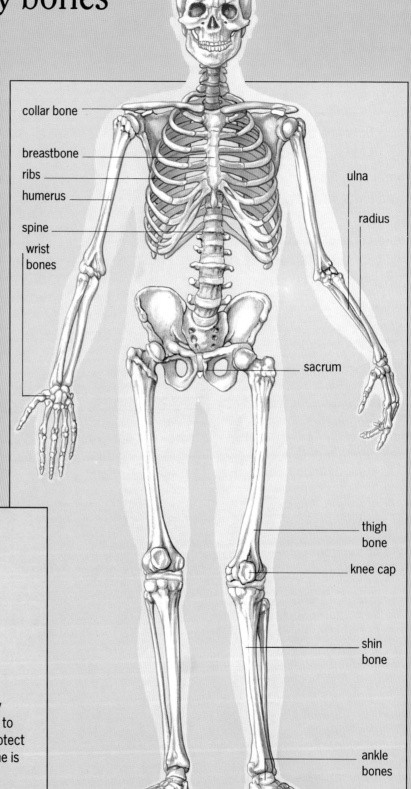

skull
collar bone
breastbone
ribs
humerus
spine
wrist bones
ulna
radius
sacrum
thigh bone
knee cap
shin bone
ankle bones

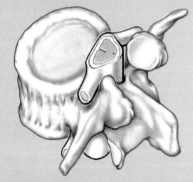

Your spine is made up of many knobbly bones called vertebrae. They allow you to bend and twist your back. They also protect the nerves of your spinal cord. The spine is also called the vertebral column.

Are my bones hollow or solid?

Bones are not hollow but they are much lighter inside than their tough, hard outer covering. The inside is spongy and criss-crossed with fine rods that make it very strong, like the struts and girders of a bridge. The spongy bone can absorb sudden shocks without cracking or breaking. The center of some bones is filled with red, jelly-like marrow. New red blood cells are made here.

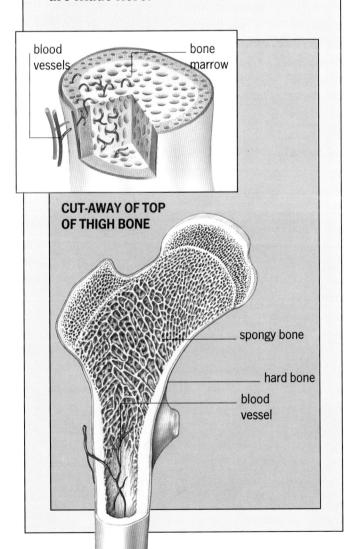

blood vessels

bone marrow

CUT-AWAY OF TOP OF THIGH BONE

spongy bone

hard bone

blood vessel

How do broken bones mend?

A broken bone repairs itself. First, marrow and blood ooze from the center of the bone into the break. Slowly new bone begins to grow across the gap. Finally the new bone hardens, welding the broken ends together.

Before the break begins to mend, a doctor will make sure that the two ends of the bone are in the correct position. A plaster cast around the break protects the bone while healing.

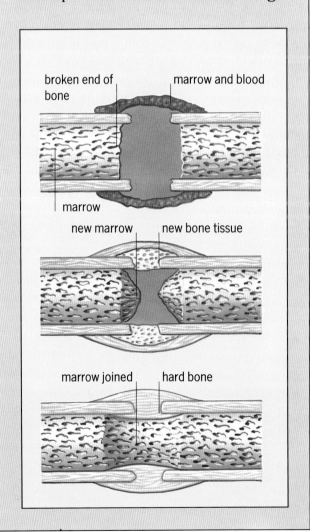

broken end of bone

marrow and blood

marrow

new marrow

new bone tissue

marrow joined

hard bone

What is the brain-box?

The brain-box is the bony armor that surrounds and protects your brain. It is made up of 21 bones fused together (at "sutures") for extra strength. Your skull bones are just under your skin, so it is easy to feel them with your fingers. There are holes through the bones of your face for your eyes, nostrils, mouth and ears. The jaw bones house your teeth. The lower jaw is the only bone in the skull that you can move.

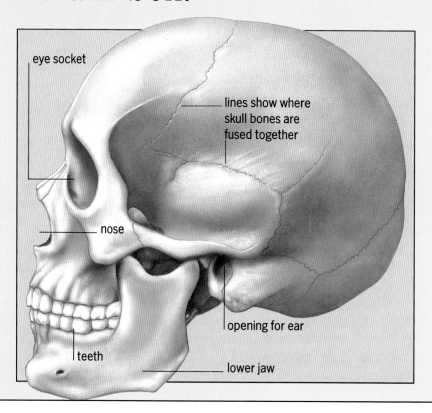

eye socket

lines show where skull bones are fused together

nose

opening for ear

teeth

lower jaw

Can bones bend?

Individual bones can bend, but only a little. You can bend your arms and legs freely because they are made up of several bones linked together. In each arm, three main bones meet and hinge at the elbow joint. Separate bones and hinge joints in your fingers allow you to move these too.

WHAT IS THE FUNNY BONE?

Sometimes, if you bang your elbow in a particular spot, a sharp pain shoots up your arm. Do not blame the bone, however, but the nerves that pass over the bone at that point. Because the nerves are unprotected by fat, they react sharply to even a small jolt.

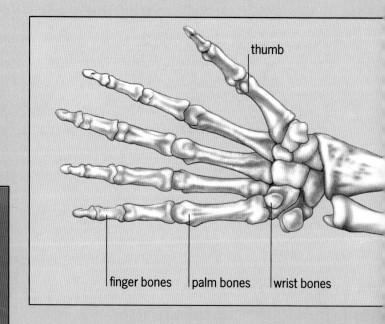

thumb

finger bones

palm bones

wrist bones

How do bones grow?

Bones develop as cartilage – a sort of rubbery material. Baby's bones are soft and bendy because they are still mainly cartilage. Calcium makes our bones hard. A baby's bones absorb calcium from milk and become harder too. Long bones grow from the ends, where cartilage slowly forms hard bone.

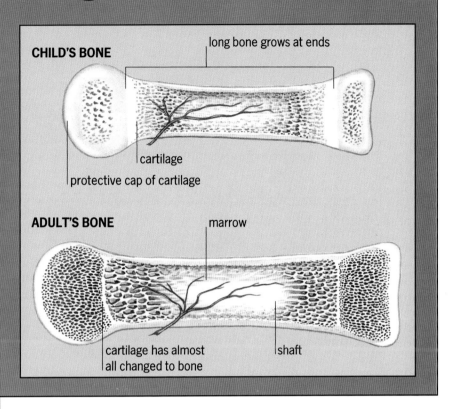

CHILD'S BONE

long bone grows at ends

cartilage

protective cap of cartilage

ADULT'S BONE

marrow

cartilage has almost all changed to bone

shaft

DID YOU KNOW...
● Most of your bones harden as you grow older, except in your ears and at the end of your nose? This remains as cartilage and you can bend and wobble it with your fingers.
● Weight for weight, bone is as strong as steel?
● A racing driver who crashed his car at 104 mph (173 km/h) broke 29 bones and dislocated 3 joints – but survived?

WHAT HOLDS BONES TOGETHER?
Tough strips of material called ligaments hold the joints together. They stretch across the joint and stop it moving too far in the wrong direction.

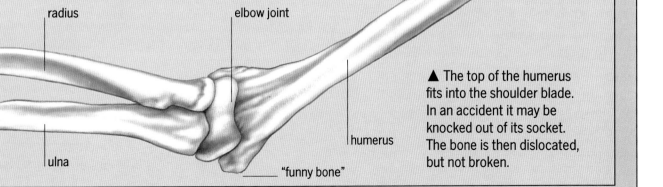

radius

elbow joint

ulna

"funny bone"

humerus

▲ The top of the humerus fits into the shoulder blade. In an accident it may be knocked out of its socket. The bone is then dislocated, but not broken.

Why can't I swivel my knee?

You can't twist your knee like you can your ankle or hip because your knee moves only one way – backward and forward in a hinge joint. Fingers and toes also have hinge joints, but not your thumb. You can rotate your thumb and bend it in any direction because it has a special joint called a saddle joint, which looks like a horse's saddle.

Joints occur wherever two bones meet. Different kinds of joints allow different kinds of movement. At the same time they are strong enough to withstand stresses and strains. The bones are held together by ligaments – strong straps of tissue. Exercise will stretch the ligaments and make the joints more flexible. To keep the joint working smoothly it is oiled by a slippery liquid called synovial fluid.

DID YOU KNOW...

● You are about .4 in (1 cm) taller when you wake up than when you went to sleep? During the day the cartilage between the vertebrae of your spine squashes together. At night it bounces back to shape.

● Girls usually have a longer forefinger than ring finger? In boys it is the other way round.

● The very last bone in your spine is known as the coccyx?

● In spite of their long necks, giraffes have no more neck-bones than we do?

● The human skull is made up of 22 separate bones? At birth, there are spaces between the bones, which later fuse together.

● Bones contain phosphorus, magnesium, fluorine, chlorine and iron as well as calcium? Your body contains enough phosphorus to make 200 match-heads and enough iron for a nail 6 in (15 cm) long?

● Teeth and bones contain calcium. They are the last to decay after death and some bones have survived for thousands of years?

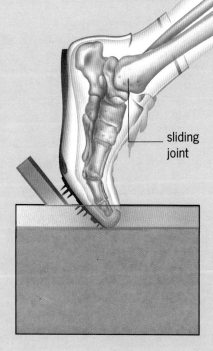

sliding joint

SLIDING JOINT
Wrists and ankles have sliding joints. They allow your hand and foot to move from side to side as well as backward and forward.

BALL AND SOCKET
Your shoulder is a ball and socket joint. It lets you swing your arm freely in any direction. The hip is also a ball and socket joint.

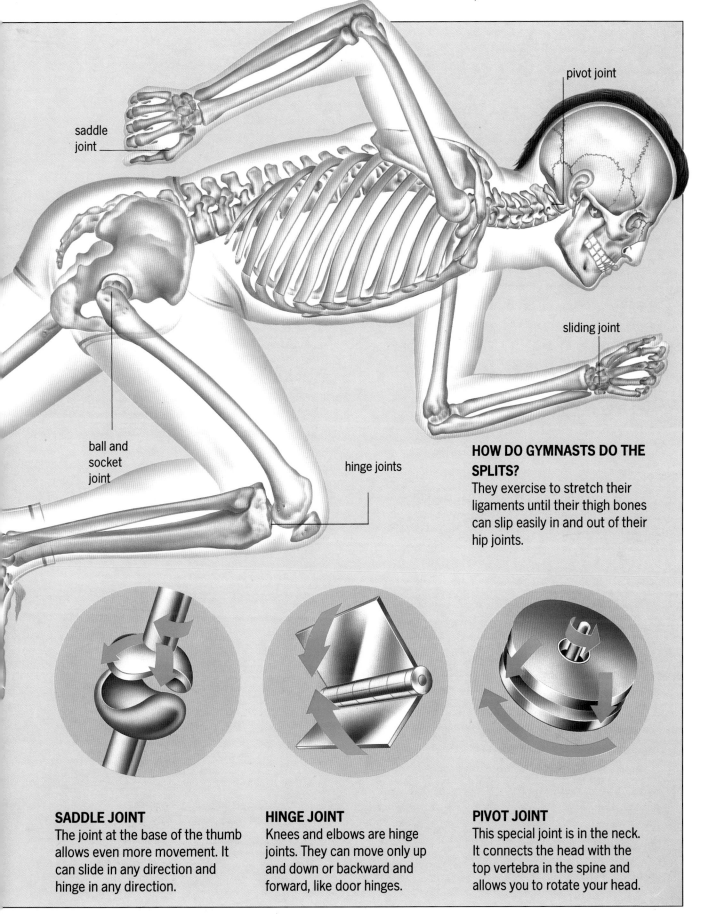

pivot joint

saddle joint

sliding joint

ball and socket joint

hinge joints

HOW DO GYMNASTS DO THE SPLITS?
They exercise to stretch their ligaments until their thigh bones can slip easily in and out of their hip joints.

SADDLE JOINT
The joint at the base of the thumb allows even more movement. It can slide in any direction and hinge in any direction.

HINGE JOINT
Knees and elbows are hinge joints. They can move only up and down or backward and forward, like door hinges.

PIVOT JOINT
This special joint is in the neck. It connects the head with the top vertebra in the spine and allows you to rotate your head.

13

How do muscles get bigger?

Bend one arm and clench your fist, holding the upper arm with your other hand. Can you feel the muscles tightening? Weight-lifters have such big muscles they bulge out. They make their muscles bigger by exercising.

You have about 650 muscles and each one produces a particular movement. Even a simple action like walking uses more than 200 muscles. But you do not need to have big, bulgy muscles for your body to work well. The muscles that move the body are anchored to your bones. A tendon joins the muscle to the bone it controls. As the muscle shortens and tightens, the tendon pulls the bone up. The more you use a muscle, the bigger and better it gets. So if you want strong muscles – exercise them!

There are some muscles that work automatically. Your heart is a muscle that pumps blood all the time. Food is pushed through your body by special muscles in your intestines.

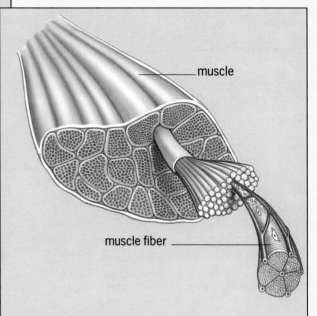

muscle

muscle fiber

WHAT ARE MUSCLES MADE OF?
Muscles are made up of bundles of elastic fibers. Each fiber is about 1.6 in (40 mm) long and consists of many tiny strands called fibrils. Fibers are very thin – .16 sq in (1 sq cm) of muscle could contain up to a million fibers. Each fiber is controlled by a nerve that makes it contract. How strongly a muscle works depends on how many fibers contract.

WHAT IS A CRAMP?
A cramp occurs when a muscle suddenly contracts unexpectedly. It is very painful and may last several minutes before the muscle relaxes again.

radius   ulna

▶ The muscles that work your fingers are in your lower arm. You can see the tendons that join them to the bones on the back of your hand. Bend a finger and feel the tendon move.

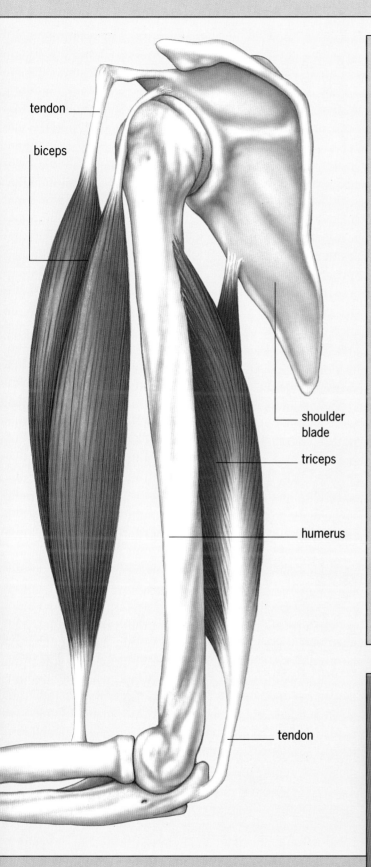

tendon

biceps

shoulder
blade

triceps

humerus

tendon

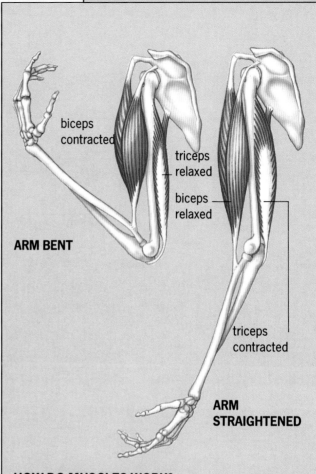

biceps
contracted

triceps
relaxed

biceps
relaxed

ARM BENT

triceps
contracted

**ARM
STRAIGHTENED**

HOW DO MUSCLES WORK?

Muscles work by pulling on a bone – they cannot push. At least two separate muscles are needed to move a joint. When the biceps contracts it raises the lower arm, while the triceps relaxes. The biceps cannot straighten the arm again. The triceps does that by pulling the ulna down while the biceps relaxes.

DID YOU KNOW...

● You use over 40 muscles when you frown, but only 15 when you smile? Be lazy – keep smiling!

● About 40 percent of your weight is due to muscle? Muscles give your body its bulk and shape.

● The biggest muscle is the gluteus maximus, or buttock? It helps you to stand up and gives you something soft to sit on!

What are teeth made of?

Most of a tooth consists of dentine, which is harder than bone. The dentine is covered with enamel – the hardest and toughest substance in the body. Teeth have to be hard because they have a tough job to do – biting and chewing food. Humans have only two sets. By the age of 3 you probably had all 20 of your milk teeth. These are gradually replaced by 32 permanent, or adult, teeth which have to last your whole life.

But teeth can decay quickly. Sugar is the worst enemy. Sugar and left-over food are eaten by bacteria in your mouth and changed into acid. Acid eats away the enamel and then the dentine below. The way to stop it is to clean your teeth often and always after eating sweet things.

HOW ARE ANIMAL TEETH DIFFERENT FROM OURS?

● Sharks go through many sets of teeth in their life. Whenever a tooth wears out, it is replaced by another.
● Rodent's teeth never stop growing. If mice, gerbils and hamsters did not chew all the time, their teeth would get ever longer.
● A walrus's tusks are two long teeth. They use them to dig shellfish out of the shingle on the seabed.
● Animals that eat only meat have mainly canine and incisor teeth. Animals that eat only plants have mainly molars.
● Crocodiles allow their teeth to be cleaned by birds called plovers.
● George Washington, the first president of the United States, had a set of false teeth carved from hippopotamus ivory.
● Kittens have teeth when they are born. Human babies also have teeth, but they are hidden in the gum. Some babies are born with a tooth in place, but it usually falls out. Most babies get their first tooth when they are 5 months old.

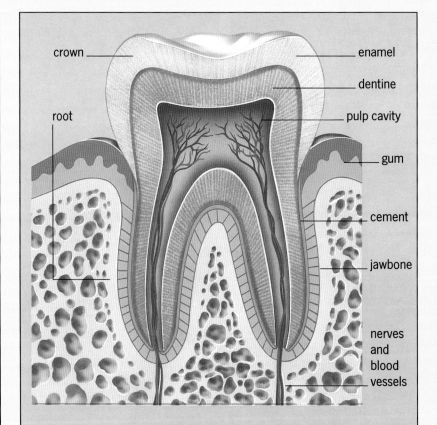

WHAT CAUSES TOOTHACHE?
The center of a tooth is filled with a soft pulp cavity. The hard outer layers of enamel and dentine have no nerves, so you feel no pain when they decay. But the pulp cavity is kept alive by blood and nerves. If a tooth is allowed to decay until the hole reaches the pulp cavity, it will cause extreme pain. You can make sure this does not happen by having your teeth regularly checked by a dentist.

What are slicers and chewers?

The different shapes of tooth have different names according to the way you use them. The flat, sharp front teeth are good for biting or slicing. They are called incisors and they work like a pair of scissors. The four fang-like teeth on either side of the incisors are the canines. They grip the food and are good for tearing meat off a bone. At the back of your mouth are premolars and large, flat molars. As you chew, they grind the food into smaller pieces, ready to be mixed with and moistened by saliva, and swallowed.

WHAT MAKES MILK TEETH FALL OUT?

Your teeth are usually firmly rooted in sockets in your jaw and held in place by a thin layer of cement. This stops them moving around as you chew. When you are about 6 or 7 years old your permanent teeth begin to grow bigger and to push up through your gums. At the same time the roots of the milk teeth begin to dissolve. The teeth get looser and looser until they just fall out. Although the milk teeth all appear within about 2 years, the permanent teeth take up to 20 years to appear, since wisdom teeth come in much later.

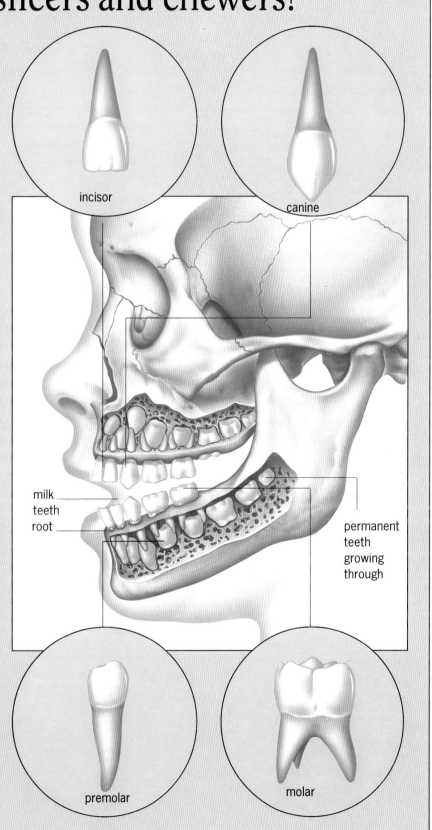

incisor

canine

milk
teeth
root

permanent
teeth
growing
through

premolar

molar

How big is my stomach?

An adult's stomach holds about a quart of food, a child's stomach probably a bit less. The food stays in your stomach for about 3 hours where it is churned around and mixed with acidic juices until it becomes a mushy soup. Your body needs food to move, grow and stay alive, but it cannot use it in the form you eat it. Food must first be broken down into tiny particles that can be absorbed into your blood. The mushy soup passes from the stomach into the long tube called the intestines. Here digestive juices break it down still more. What is not absorbed from the intestines goes on through the gut to the rectum.

The back of your throat opens into two pipes. One takes food to the stomach and the other, the windpipe, takes air to the lungs. A flap of cartilage called the epiglottis ensures that food does not go down the wrong pipe. It closes off the windpipe when you swallow.

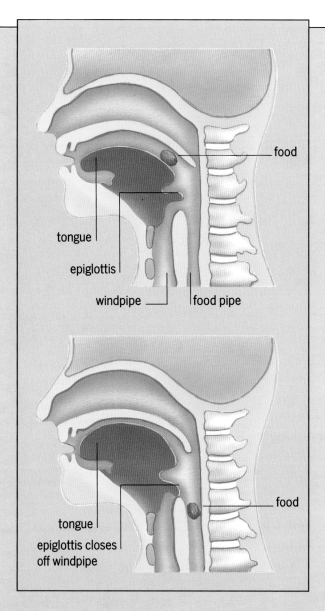

food

tongue

epiglottis

windpipe | food pipe

food

tongue

epiglottis closes off windpipe

Can you swallow when upside-down?

Take a mouthful of water, bend over to touch the floor, then swallow. The water runs uphill to your stomach! Food is pushed through your body, not by gravity, but by circular and longitudinal muscles in the walls of your gut.

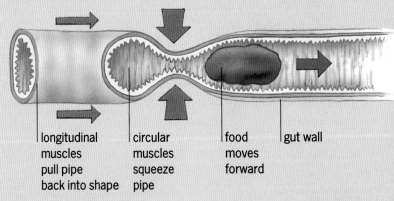

longitudinal muscles pull pipe back into shape | circular muscles squeeze pipe | food moves forward | gut wall

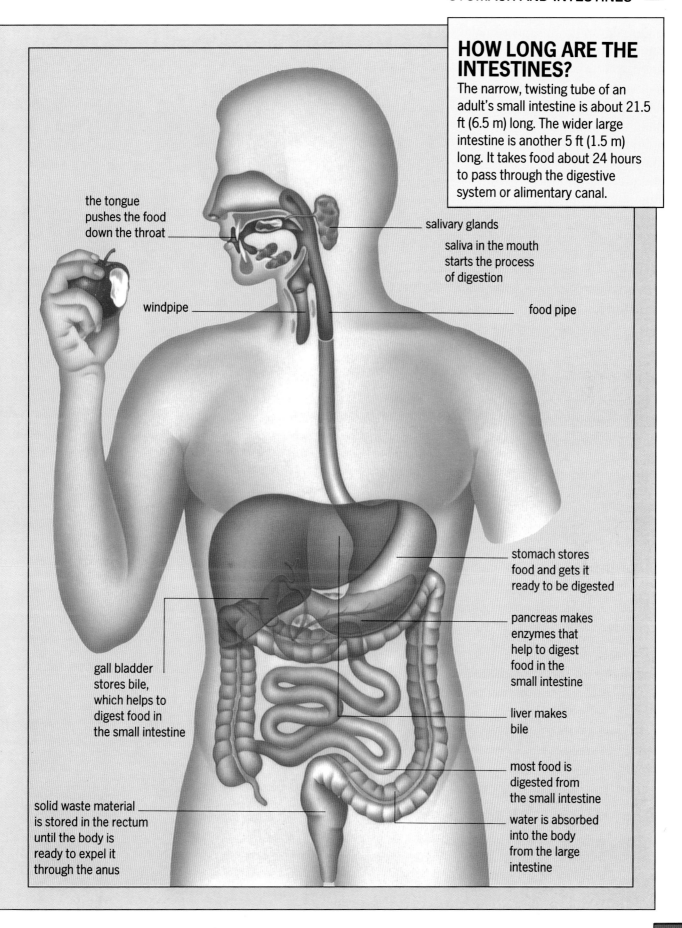

HOW LONG ARE THE INTESTINES?

The narrow, twisting tube of an adult's small intestine is about 21.5 ft (6.5 m) long. The wider large intestine is another 5 ft (1.5 m) long. It takes food about 24 hours to pass through the digestive system or alimentary canal.

the tongue pushes the food down the throat

salivary glands

saliva in the mouth starts the process of digestion

windpipe

food pipe

stomach stores food and gets it ready to be digested

pancreas makes enzymes that help to digest food in the small intestine

gall bladder stores bile, which helps to digest food in the small intestine

liver makes bile

most food is digested from the small intestine

solid waste material is stored in the rectum until the body is ready to expel it through the anus

water is absorbed into the body from the large intestine

How does digested food reach the blood?

The inside of the small intestine is lined with thousands of tiny finger-like lumps called villi. Just under the skin of each villus are many minute blood vessels. The food you eat is slowly broken down into microscopic molecules, so small that they can slide between the cells of the villi skin and into the blood vessels. The food is then absorbed into the blood.

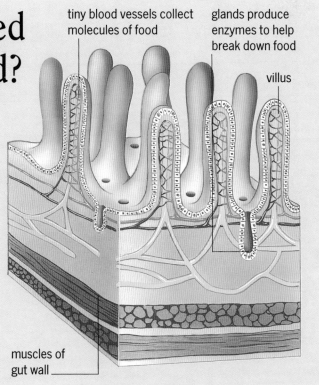

tiny blood vessels collect molecules of food

glands produce enzymes to help break down food

villus

muscles of gut wall

▶ Most food is broken down and digested in the small intestine. It is lined with thousands of tiny villi, which have been magnified here many hundreds of times.

What is pee?

Pee, or urine, is water mixed with poisonous waste produced by your body. Blood takes food to every part of your body and collects poisons and waste products at the same time. As the blood passes through the liver and then the kidneys, the poisons are removed and mixed with water to make urine. Urine trickles down to the balloon-like bladder where it is stored.

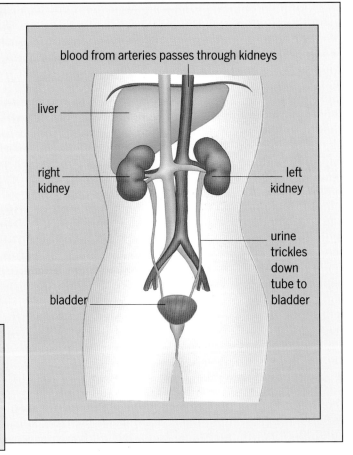

blood from arteries passes through kidneys

liver

right kidney

left kidney

urine trickles down tube to bladder

bladder

WHAT MAKES ME PEE?

When the bladder is full, nerves send a message to the brain that you need to pee. If you drink lots of liquid the bladder fills up quickly and the urine is weaker.

What does the liver do?

You can survive without a stomach, but no one can live without a liver. It does many essential jobs. The blood vessels that collect food from the intestines join a large vein that takes all the blood and food to the liver. The liver checks the contents. If there is too much sugar, it removes the extra and stores it, either in the liver itself or as fat elsewhere in the body. It also stores vitamins and changes fats and proteins into forms in which they can be used. It extracts poisons and sends them to the kidneys. It makes sure your body gets just the nutrients it needs.

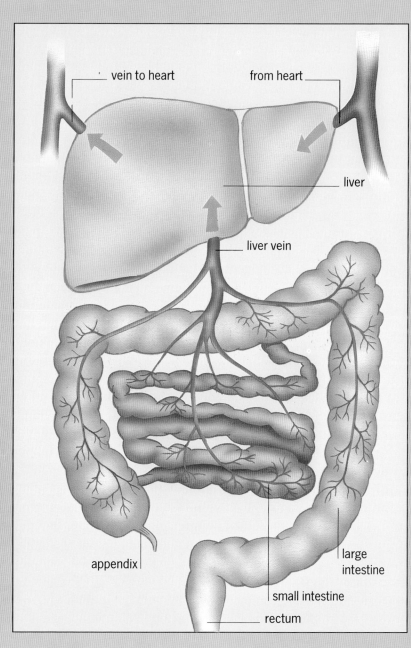

vein to heart

from heart

liver

liver vein

appendix

small intestine

rectum

large intestine

DID YOU KNOW...

● The liver is the biggest gland in the body? It is bigger than the stomach and accounts for 4 percent of the weight of a child.

● The liver can renew itself? If three-quarters were removed, the rest would not only go on working on its own but also would soon have grown as large as the whole liver used to be.

● People used to think the liver was the most important part of the body? They called it the seat of life and thought that your mood was controlled by the liver.

● Your appendix is of no use to you at all, but sometimes it becomes inflamed and very painful and has to be removed?

● About a quarter of all your blood is pumped through your kidneys every minute?

● You normally pee about a quart to 1.5 quarts of urine a day?

● You pee less in hot weather when your body loses more water in sweat?

● Your bladder stretches like a balloon as it fills up with urine? You usually need to pee when it contains about 15.25 cubic inches (250 cc) of urine.

How much air do lungs hold?

Adult lungs hold about 5 quarts of air, children's around 3 quarts. You do not empty and fill your lungs every time you breathe. When you are sitting quietly you breathe in less than 30.5 cubic inches (500 cc) of air. Air passes through your nose or mouth into the windpipe and bronchii, then into the lungs. In the lungs the oxygen is absorbed through tiny air sacs into your blood. At the same time the waste gas carbon dioxide leaves the blood and joins the air you breathe out.

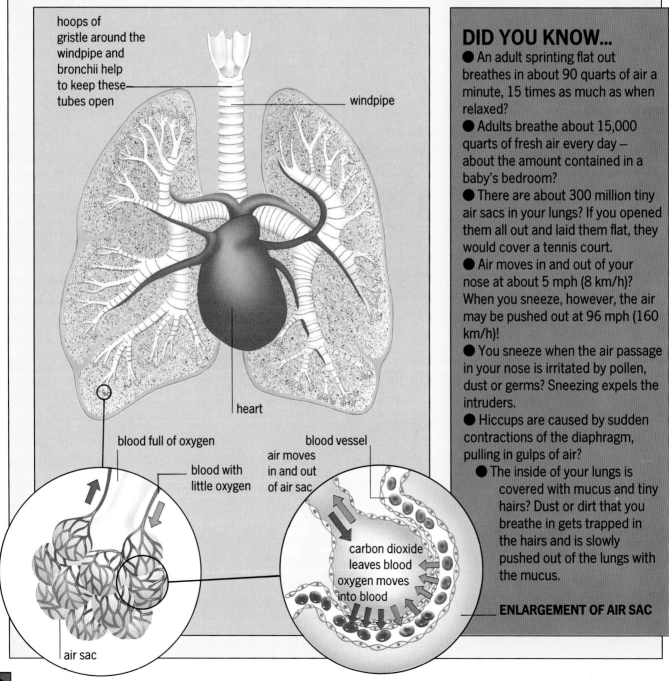

hoops of gristle around the windpipe and bronchii help to keep these tubes open

windpipe

heart

blood full of oxygen

blood with little oxygen

blood vessel
air moves in and out of air sac

carbon dioxide leaves blood oxygen moves into blood

air sac

DID YOU KNOW...

● An adult sprinting flat out breathes in about 90 quarts of air a minute, 15 times as much as when relaxed?

● Adults breathe about 15,000 quarts of fresh air every day — about the amount contained in a baby's bedroom?

● There are about 300 million tiny air sacs in your lungs? If you opened them all out and laid them flat, they would cover a tennis court.

● Air moves in and out of your nose at about 5 mph (8 km/h)? When you sneeze, however, the air may be pushed out at 96 mph (160 km/h)!

● You sneeze when the air passage in your nose is irritated by pollen, dust or germs? Sneezing expels the intruders.

● Hiccups are caused by sudden contractions of the diaphragm, pulling in gulps of air?

● The inside of your lungs is covered with mucus and tiny hairs? Dust or dirt that you breathe in gets trapped in the hairs and is slowly pushed out of the lungs with the mucus.

ENLARGEMENT OF AIR SAC

How often do I need to breathe?

When you are relaxed you may need to breathe only around 15 times a minute, but when you are running around your body needs much more air, making you pant and gasp. Your lungs suck in air when the rib muscles and the diaphragm contract and push out your ribs. As these relax they push the air out of the lungs.

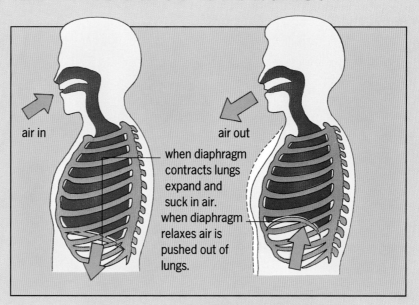

air in

air out

when diaphragm contracts lungs expand and suck in air. when diaphragm relaxes air is pushed out of lungs.

How do I talk?

The voice box is at the top of your windpipe. As you breathe out the air passes through the voice box and vibrates the vocal cords. When you breathe without speaking the gap between the vocal cords is large. It narrows to make different sounds when you speak. To make all the sounds you need for words involves moving your lips, tongue and teeth too.

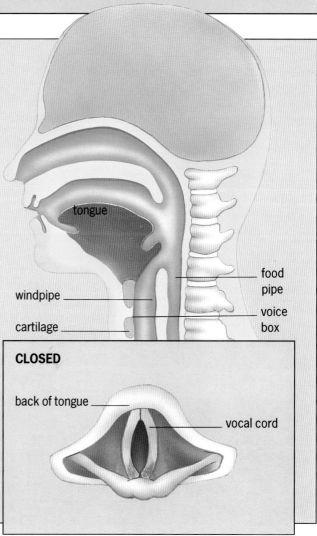

tongue

windpipe

cartilage

food pipe

voice box

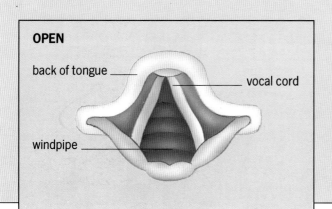

OPEN

back of tongue

vocal cord

windpipe

CLOSED

back of tongue

vocal cord

How much blood do I have?

Adults have between 5 and 6 quarts of blood. Children have less depending on their size. Blood travels around your body nearly 2,000 times every day. It is pumped around by the heart, a muscle about the size of your fist. Blood leaves the heart and lungs in large arteries that divide into narrower and narrower tubes. Tiny capillaries, no thicker than a hair, feed every living part of the body with food and oxygen. More capillaries take the used blood and carbon dioxide back to the veins and then to the heart and lungs for recirculating.

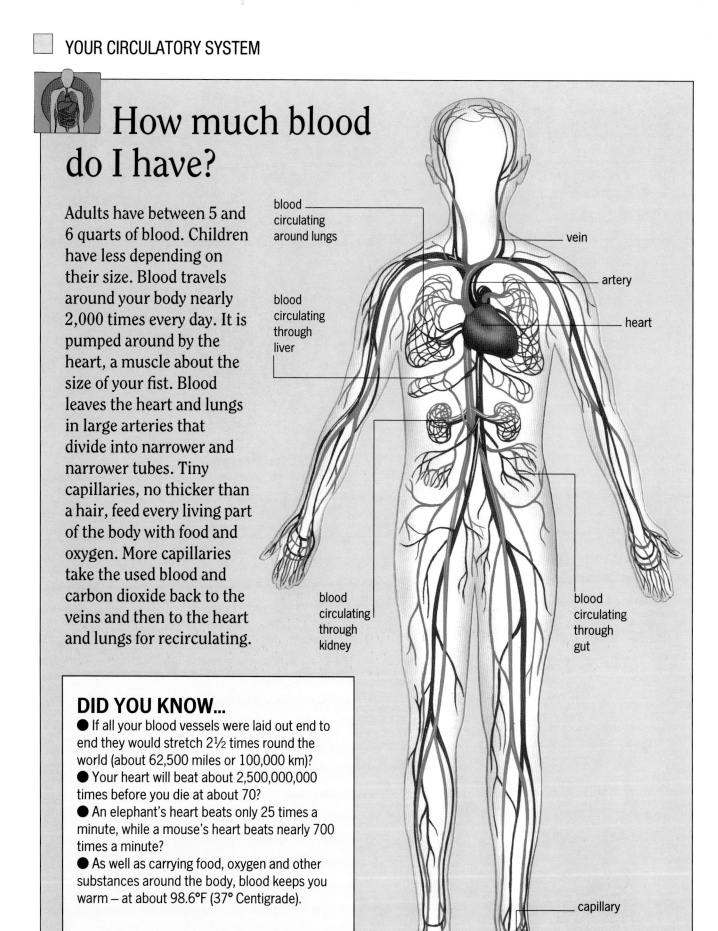

blood circulating around lungs

blood circulating through liver

vein

artery

heart

blood circulating through kidney

blood circulating through gut

capillary

DID YOU KNOW...

● If all your blood vessels were laid out end to end they would stretch 2½ times round the world (about 62,500 miles or 100,000 km)?

● Your heart will beat about 2,500,000,000 times before you die at about 70?

● An elephant's heart beats only 25 times a minute, while a mouse's heart beats nearly 700 times a minute?

● As well as carrying food, oxygen and other substances around the body, blood keeps you warm – at about 98.6°F (37° Centigrade).

How often does my heart beat?

Your heart probably beats about 80 times a minute. Adult hearts beat slightly slower – about 70 times a minute when relaxing. When the heart beats, it contracts and squeezes blood into the arteries. When the muscles of the heart relax, more blood pours in from the veins. The heart is actually two pumps. One pump sends some of the blood to the lungs to collect oxygen, while the other sends blood to the rest of the body. When you exercise and make your muscles work harder, your heart beats faster to supply those muscles with more than 21 quarts of blood a minute.

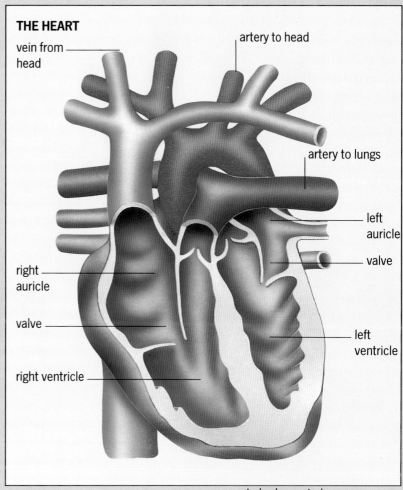

THE HEART

vein from head

artery to head

artery to lungs

left auricle

valve

right auricle

valve

left ventricle

right ventricle

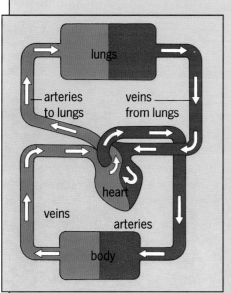

lungs

arteries to lungs

veins from lungs

heart

veins

arteries

body

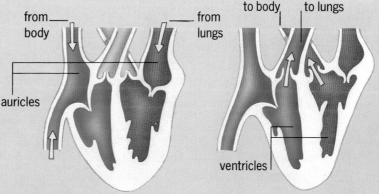

from body

from lungs

to body

to lungs

auricles

ventricles

The right half of the heart receives blood from the body and sends it to the lungs. The left half receives oxygen-filled blood from the lungs and sends it to the rest of the body. As blood enters the auricles, the heart contracts and squeezes it into the ventricles below. Valves between auricles and ventricles control the direction of the flow of the blood and prevent any backflow.

Why is blood red?

A tiny drop of blood, no more than a small fraction of an inch, contains up to 5 million red blood cells, which give your blood its color. The red cells contain hemoglobin and oxygen. When the oxygen has been used by the body, the red cells change from bright red to dark red, not to blue as usually shown on diagrams. The same drop of blood also contains 7,500 white blood cells, which kill invading germs, and 250,000 platelets, which help blood to clot.

WHAT MAKES BLOOD RUNNY?

More than half of the blood is liquid plasma. Nine-tenths of plasma is simply water, while the other tenth is mainly dissolved food.

plasma

wall of blood vessel

red blood cell

HOT OR COLD?

Your blood helps to keep your body at the right temperature. When you get too hot, the tiny blood vessels near the surface of the skin stretch. More blood reaches the surface to be cooled. You can see this happening because your skin gets redder. But when you are cold, the same small blood vessels get narrower. This stops blood coming to the surface and keeps its heat in. At the same time your skin gets paler and you may start to shiver.

PALE WITH COLD **FLUSHED WITH HEAT**

DID YOU KNOW...

● You probably have a total of about 15 trillion red blood cells, 20 billion white blood cells and 700 billion platelets in your body?

● Red cells live only for a month or two, so your bone marrow has to manufacture about 100 million new red cells every minute?

● Each red blood cell contains about 280 million molecules of hemoglobin? Hemoglobin absorbs oxygen and carries it around the body. It also contains iron. The oxygen and iron together make blood red.

● In the past people thought that bleeding or "blood-letting" helped to cure disease? They attached leeches to their skin to do the job for them. Only the leeches benefited!

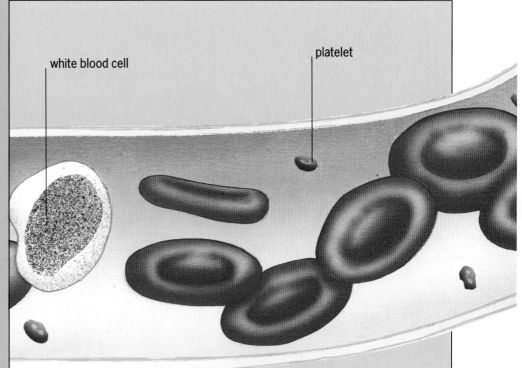

white blood cell

platelet

HOW DO WHITE CELLS WORK?
When white blood cells meet germs, they swallow them up and destroy them. They often die in the process. White cells are much bigger than red blood cells.

WHAT ARE ANTIBODIES?
When your body becomes infected, the spleen makes antibodies to counteract the germs. Antibodies help white blood cells kill germs.

WHAT IS MY BLOOD GROUP?
We do not all have exactly the same kind of blood. There are four different blood groups — A, B, AB and O. Sometimes people need a blood transfusion. Then it is important to know which blood groups can mix together. Group O can be given to every other group, but can receive only group O. Group AB can receive any other blood group, but can give only to group AB. The diagram shows which groups A and B can give to and receive from. Individuals receiving blood are called recipients. Those that give their blood for others are donors.

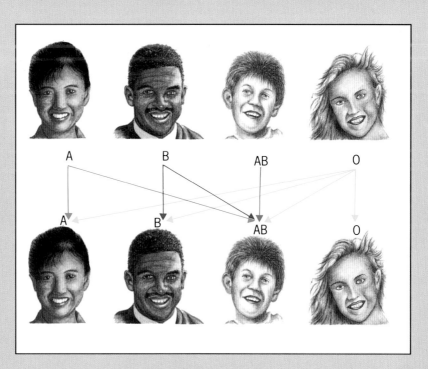

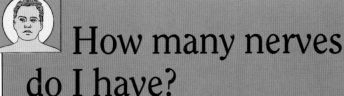

How many nerves do I have?

You have billions of nerves that go all over your body. Nerves carry tiny electric impulses to and from your brain. The brain does not look very special, but this soft, pink lump is the control center for the whole body. It contains 14 billion cells and millions of nerve fibers. It receives information from your eyes, ears, skin, mouth and nose. It controls all your muscles. It sends messages along your nerves to keep your heart beating, your lungs breathing and is ready to trigger other muscles.

DID YOU KNOW...
● Electric impulses travel along the nerves at up to 240 mph (400 km/h)? Many can pass along nerves each second.
● Nerve fibers are very fine – a hundred laid side by side would measure just 0.4 in (1 mm)?
● When brain cells die or are destroyed, they cannot be replaced?
● The lefthand side of the brain controls the right side of the body?

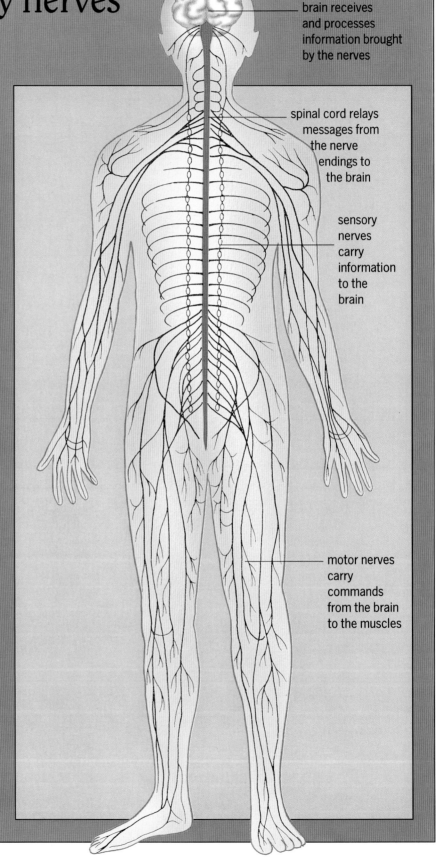

brain receives and processes information brought by the nerves

spinal cord relays messages from the nerve endings to the brain

sensory nerves carry information to the brain

motor nerves carry commands from the brain to the muscles

How does my brain work?

Your brain receives information, and interprets it. Messages flash from one part of the brain to another. Each part has its own job. The outer layer is called the cortex. It is deeply grooved. Different parts deal just with seeing, or movement or thinking.

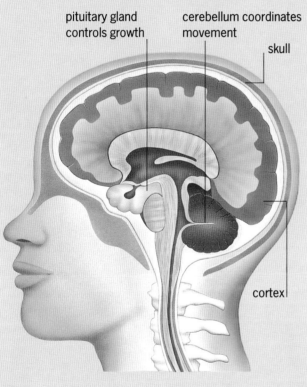

pituitary gland controls growth

cerebellum coordinates movement

skull

cortex

THE CORTEX

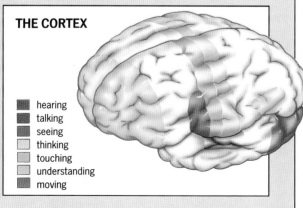

- hearing
- talking
- seeing
- thinking
- touching
- understanding
- moving

Does the brain ever rest?

No. Parts of your brain work all the time without your knowing it. These parts control your heartbeat and keep organs such as your liver working. The nerves that control these organs work in pairs. One set makes them work faster, the other slower.

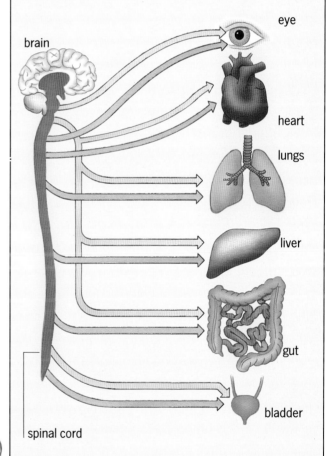

brain

eye

heart

lungs

liver

gut

bladder

spinal cord

The diagram shows how the nerves work on other organs. Even when you are asleep or unconscious, part of your brain is sending out signals.

What's inside my eye?

Each of your eyes measures almost .8 in (2 cm) across and consists mostly of jelly. The jelly keeps your eye in the correct shape so that when light passes through the pupil and lens it falls on the right part of the retina at the back of the eye.

The pupil, lens and retina work rather like a camera. The colored iris around the pupil makes it larger or smaller to let in the right amount of light. The lens focuses the light to make a clear image on the retina. The retina is not celluloid film, but contains about 130 million nerve cells. When light falls on any one of them it sends an electric impulse along the nerve to the brain. Although the image of what you see is formed upside-down on the retina, the brain turns it the right way up in your mind!

The front of your eye is protected by a transparent shield called the cornea. Eyelids, eyelashes and tears also protect your eye. If anything comes close to your eye, you blink before you know it!

WHAT ARE TEARS?

Every time you blink, each eyelid washes the cornea with salty water to keep it moist and clean. It is difficult to keep your eyes open even for a minute without blinking! Tears are made by a gland above each eye and they usually drain away into your nose, but sometimes your eyes produce so much liquid, it overflows.

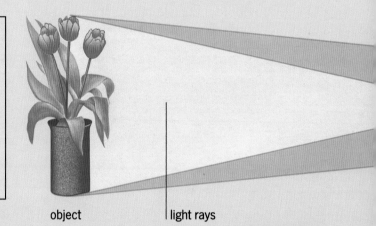

object   light rays

WHY DOES EVERYTHING LOOK GRAY AT NIGHT?

There are two kinds of nerve cells in the retina. They are called rods and cones. Cones are sensitive to different colors but rods are not. Cones need a lot of light to work well, but rods work best when there is very little light. So at night we see only in shades of gray. Rods outnumber cones by 20:1; each eye contains approximately 140 million rods and 7 million cones.

There are three kinds of cone, which react either to red, green or blue light. All the other colors are a mixture of these. Some animals, such as owls, which see well at night, have even more rods compared to cones than we do.

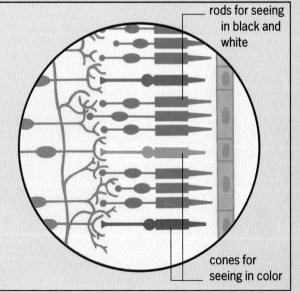

rods for seeing in black and white

cones for seeing in color

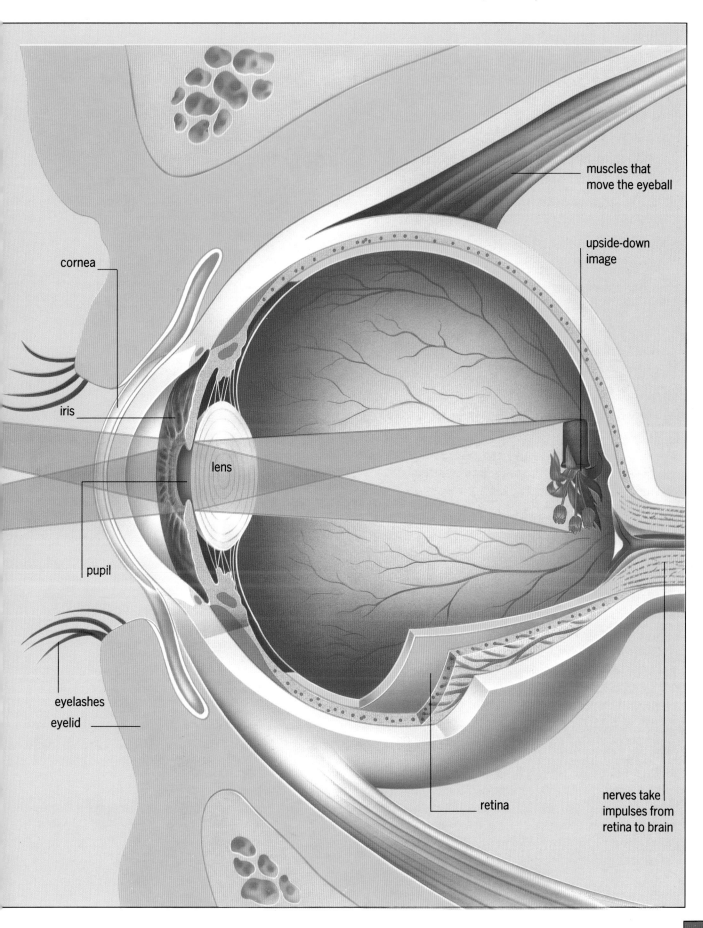

muscles that
move the eyeball

upside-down
image

cornea

iris

lens

pupil

eyelashes

eyelid

retina

nerves take
impulses from
retina to brain

How do my ears hear?

Sounds are carried to your ears as tiny vibrations in the air. If you pluck a guitar string, you can feel it vibrating. The air around it vibrates too. The vibrations pass down each ear canal to your eardrum. Just behind the eardrum are three tiny bones – the hammer, the anvil and the stirrup. They pick up and magnify the vibrations and carry them to a thin layer of skin called the oval window. It connects with the cochlea deep inside your head. The cochlea is filled with liquid and here the vibrations are changed into electric impulses and sent by nerves to the brain.

Two ears help you to tell which direction a sound is coming from, but you ignore most of what you hear! Your brain tells you which sounds to pay attention to.

HOW DO ACROBATS BALANCE SO WELL?
The inner ear also contains an organ that helps you to balance. The three semi-circular canals are all at right angles to each other. They are filled with liquid that moves as you move your body. Nerve endings keep your brain informed of your exact position. Acrobats train themselves to be aware of the slightest change in their position for perfect balance.

WHY DO I GET DIZZY?
When you spin around and around the liquid in the semi- circular canals spins around too. This confuses your brain so the whole world seems to spin!

To overcome the problem a ballerina keeps her eyes fixed on one spot on the stage. As she spins her body, she keeps her head still for most of the turn, then jerks it around.

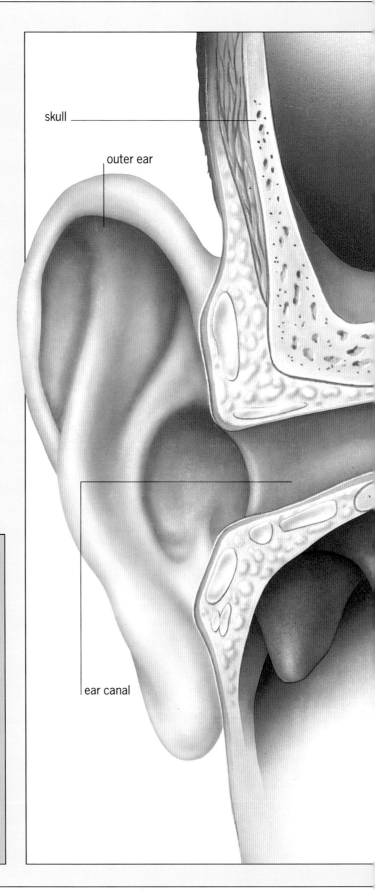

skull

outer ear

ear canal

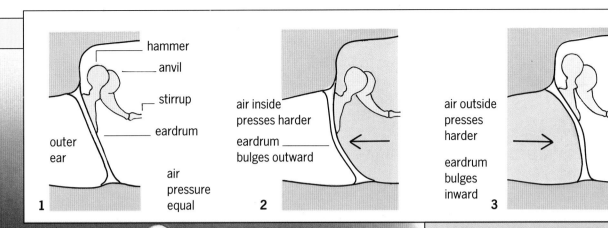

1 outer ear · hammer · anvil · stirrup · eardrum · air pressure equal

2 air inside presses harder · eardrum bulges outward

3 air outside presses harder · eardrum bulges inward

semi-circular canals

inner ear

nerves carry impulses to brain

eardrum

oval window

Eustachian tube

To the back of the nose

cochlea

WHY DO MY EARS POP?

Have you ever noticed your ears pop when you take off or land in an aircraft? There is a pocket of air inside your eardrum. If the air on one side of the eardrum presses harder than on the other side, the eardrum bulges and you cannot hear as well as usual. Only when the pressure inside and out is equal again do your ears "pop" back to normal. The air inside your ear comes from your mouth along the Eustachian tube. Swallowing helps to make your ears pop quicker.

CAN EARS GET BLOCKED?

When you have a cold, the Eustachian tubes may become blocked with mucus. You will not hear so well if the mucus reaches the eardrum and muffles its vibrations. Blowing your nose often helps to clear your ears too. Young children's ears do not always clear quickly. The mucus gets "gluey."

CAN NOISE KILL?

Noise is measured in decibels. A jet plane may reach 100 decibels and make your ears hurt. Sounds over 90 decibels can damage your hearing. Noises over 165 decibels can kill you.

WHY DO ANIMALS HEAR SO WELL?

Many animals, such as dogs, mice and cats, have big, pointy ears that they can move to catch more sound. They listen out for danger and for prey.

WHAT IS WAX FOR?

Wax, believe it or not, keeps your ears clean. Any dirt or dust that gets into the ear canal is trapped in the wax and slowly pushed out of the ear. The wax is made by the skin in the ear canal.

33

How do I smell things?

High inside your nose is a patch of nerve endings that are sensitive to smell. When you breathe normally, hardly any air touches them, but they can detect a smell from just a few tiny particles. They are covered with tiny hairs and sticky mucus. The mucus traps the smelly chemicals around the hairs. When you sniff hard, much more air is pushed straight on to these nerve endings. The nerves carry an electric impulse to the brain. Then you can tell what the smell is!

WHY CAN'T I SMELL WITH A COLD?

Most people can usually detect about 10,000 different smells. When you have a cold, a virus attacks the lining of your nose and throat and your body makes extra mucus to protect itself. If your nose is filled with mucus, no air can reach the smell detectors in your nose. Since smell and taste are linked, you can't taste either!

HOW WELL DO ANIMALS SMELL?

● Dogs can smell a million times better than humans. Like many other animals, they have longer noses and more nerve endings sensitive to smell. The nerve endings are not hidden at the top of the nose, as in humans, but placed to catch smell with every breath. Even so, dogs get their noses right down on the ground when they are following a scent.

● Dogs can follow the smell of a person's footprints over rocks, grass, mud and roads. But today police dogs are more often used for sniffing out illegal drugs than for tracking criminals.

● Pigs are used in France to sniff out truffles in the soil. The pigs find them easily, not only because they have a good sense of smell, but because they like to eat them too!

● The male emperor moth has the best sense of smell of all. Its feathery antennae can detect the scent of a female emperor moth up to 6.6 mi (11 km) away.

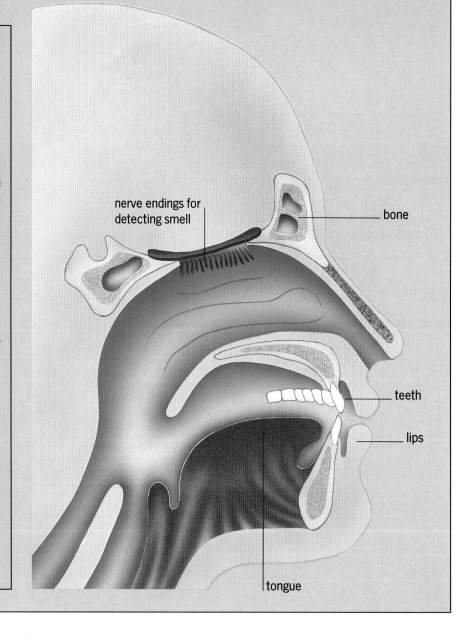

nerve endings for detecting smell

bone

teeth

lips

tongue

How do I tell smells apart?

No one knows the answer to this question, but most scientists think that there are several kinds of nerve endings for smell. Each one detects a different type of smell, such as flowery, fatty, fruity or revolting. Most smells are a combination of several types and so a diffferent combination of nerve endings tells your brain about each different smell. The olfactory or smell center of the brain interprets the signals.

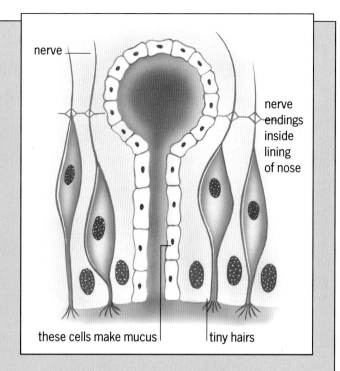

nerve

nerve endings inside lining of nose

these cells make mucus

tiny hairs

How do I taste?

If you lick chocolate with the tip of your tongue, it will taste only sweet. But when you swallow it, you will notice it has a bitter taste too. Most of your 3,000 taste buds are clustered around the edge and at

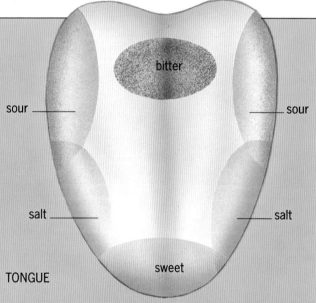

sour

bitter

sour

salt

salt

sweet

TONGUE

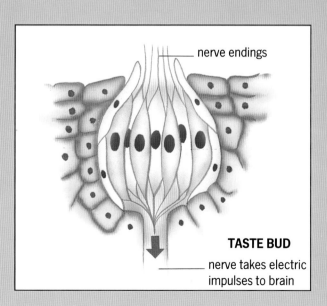

nerve endings

TASTE BUD

nerve takes electric impulses to brain

the back of your tongue. Each bud can detect only one of four basic tastes – salty, sweet, sour or bitter. Every other taste is made up of a mixture of these, which your brain learns to recognize. But you will not taste anything if your mouth is dry. The nerve endings in each taste bud react only to particles dissolved in saliva.

Why and how do we feel pain?

Pain is a warning that something is wrong. It is the quickest way of making sure the body takes action to protect itself. Special nerve endings in the skin and muscles send warning impulses to the brain when they are stimulated.

There are three levels of pain. Nerve endings nearest the surface of the skin make you feel itchy or tingling when they are lightly touched. Heavier pressure can produce a sharp pain, and injury deep in the skin will give you an aching pain.

NERVE ENDINGS IN THE SKIN

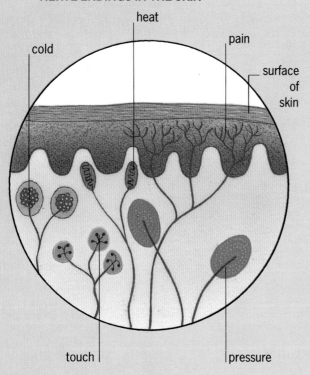

heat

cold

pain

surface of skin

touch

pressure

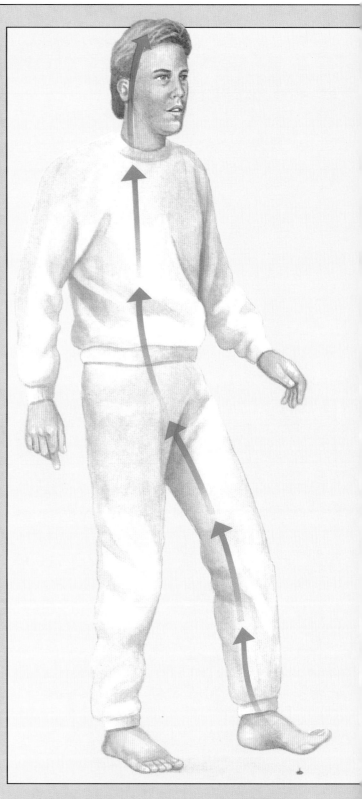

▲ Skin is sensitive to heat, cold and touch as well as pain. Each of these sensations has its own nerve endings, but they are unevenly distributed around the body. Your lips are most sensitive.

WHY ARE FINGERTIPS SO SENSITIVE?
Your fingertips are crammed full of nerve endings sensitive to touch and pain. Try feeling flat surfaces such as walls with your eyes closed. You will feel bumps you cannot see!

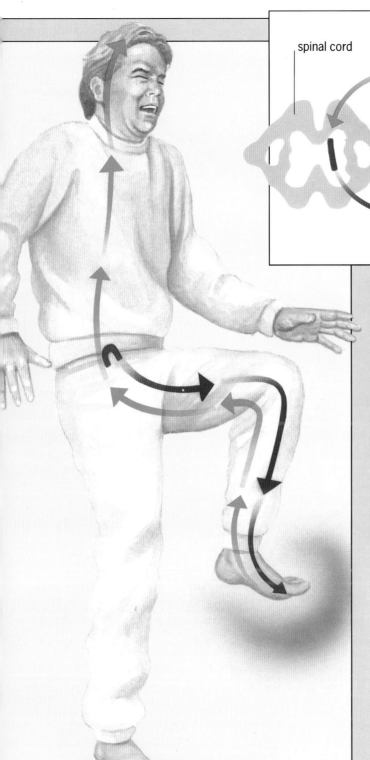

spinal cord

pain impulse from
nerve in foot

nerve impulse to
leg muscles

WHAT IS A REFLEX ACTION?

If you step on something sharp, you pull your foot
away without thinking. This is called a reflex action.
When the messages of pain reach your spinal cord,
nerve impulses are sent immediately to your leg
muscles to contract and move your foot. The pain
impulses still go on to your brain, but you probably
cry "ouch!" after the danger is over!

When you learn to do something well, it too can
become a reflex action. When you first learn to ride a
bicycle, you have to think about everything you do,
particularly your balance. But the more you practice
the easier it becomes, until you can keep your
balance automatically. Even pressing the buttons in
a computer game can become a reflex action.

WHY DOES IT HURT TO PULL MY HAIR?
Although there are no nerves in hairs, there are
nerve endings around the roots and these are
triggered when your hair is pulled. Pulling one
hair hurts more than pulling a handful!

What is a cell?

A cell is the smallest building block in the body. Most are so tiny you cannot see them without a microscope. There are many kinds of cells in the body – all of different shapes and sizes. Sperm cells have a long tail to help them swim. Red blood cells are round and flat. Brain cells have long extensions to join with each other. Each kind of cell has its own job to do. Skin cells work differently from muscle cells or nerve cells, but every cell needs food and oxygen to stay alive.

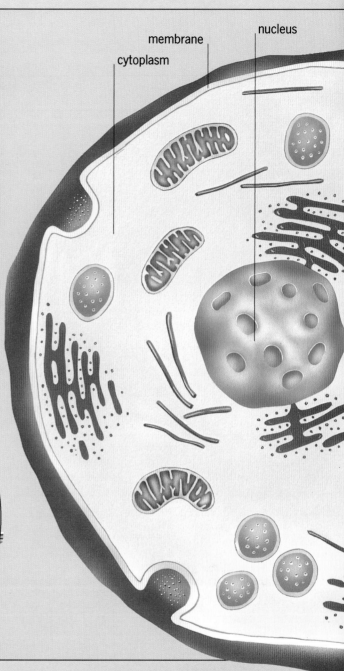

membrane

nucleus

cytoplasm

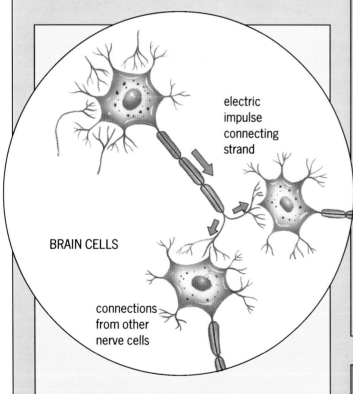

electric impulse connecting strand

BRAIN CELLS

connections from other nerve cells

HOW DO BRAIN CELLS WORK?

Many things are going on in your brain at the same time. Different parts of the brain need to communicate with each other. They do so by sending electric impulses along connecting strands to several other cells at once.

HOW LONG DO CELLS LIVE?

Most of our body cells die much quicker than we do, but do not worry – they are constantly being replaced with new ones. None of your body cells, except your brain and bone cells, was alive when you were born! Stomach cells live for only 2 days, skin cells 25 days. Some blood cells last for only 10 hours. Your brain cells cannot be renewed, but most of them will last a lifetime.

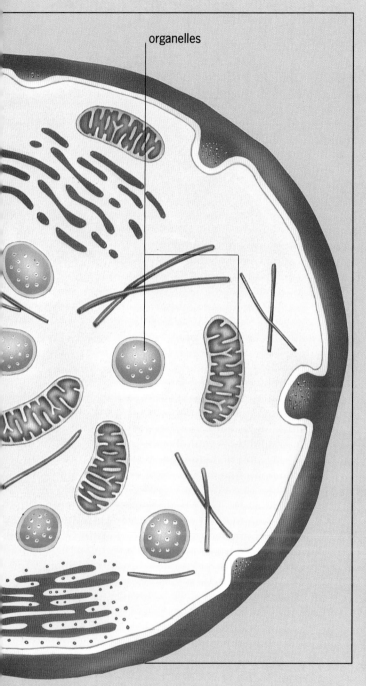

organelles

DID YOU KNOW...
● The biggest human body cells are the female sex cells? They are half the size of a grain of salt. Male sex cells are half their size. About 20 of them laid head to tail would be only .04 in (1 mm).
● Brain cells are even smaller and are among the smallest in the body? Those in the cerebellum measure only .0002 in (0.005 mm). More than 300 would fit onto this period.

What's inside a cell?
Most of the inside of a cell is "jelly" called cytoplasm. Tiny structures called organelles float around in the jelly and they do the work of the cell – turning food into energy, for example. The nucleus controls the cell. All the instructions for what the cell has to do are contained in a special code in the nucleus. The cell is surrounded by a thin skin, or membrane, which controls what enters and leaves it.

HOW DO BLOOD CELLS FIGHT DISEASE?
White blood cells flow around your body, on the lookout for germs. When an intruder is discovered, the white cell surrounds it and swallows it. One white cell can swallow several bacteria. Enzymes inside the cell kill the bacteria and the harmless remains are pushed out. White cells not only combat germs in the blood. They can change shape and slide out of a blood vessel into the surrounding tissue in search of germs. White cells consume anything that should not be in the body – dirt in the lungs, and even, though slowly, a splinter.

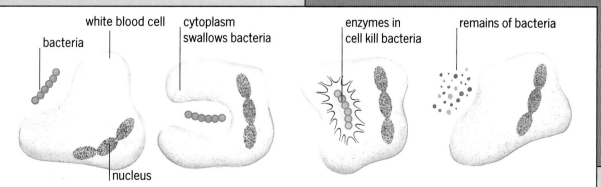

bacteria

white blood cell

cytoplasm swallows bacteria

enzymes in cell kill bacteria

remains of bacteria

nucleus

How does new life start?

When a male sperm joins with a female egg cell, the two combine to form the first cell of a new life. This is the process of fertilization. That cell divides into two again and again to form a baby. The sperm and egg cell join after sexual intercourse. During intercourse the man puts his erect penis into the woman's vagina. Millions of tiny sperm squirt from his penis and swim toward the egg cell. As soon as one sperm has entered the egg, a barrier forms around it to stop other sperm getting in.

TWINS OR TRIPLETS?

● If by chance two egg cells are fertilized, the mother will produce two babies, or twins.

● Sometimes a mother produces three, four or five babies (triplets, quadruplets and quintuplets) at the same time.

● A Russian woman in the 18th century is said to have produced 16 sets of twins, seven sets of triplets and four sets of quadruplets.

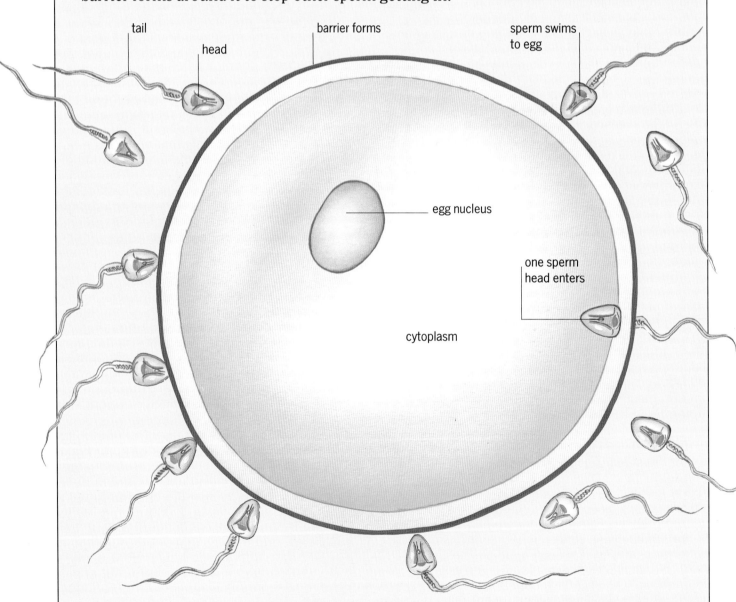

tail

head

barrier forms

sperm swims to egg

egg nucleus

one sperm head enters

cytoplasm

Where do egg cells come from?

A girl is born with over 100,000 egg cells in each of her two ovaries. When she reaches puberty, at about 12 or 13, only about 10,000 remain. Each month one egg cell ripens and makes its way down the Fallopian tubes to her uterus, or womb. Unless it is fertilized by sperm, the egg and the lining of the womb are discarded by the uterus down the vagina with some blood. This is called the period. It happens for a few days every month. Only about 450 of the eggs in a woman's ovaries will ripen.

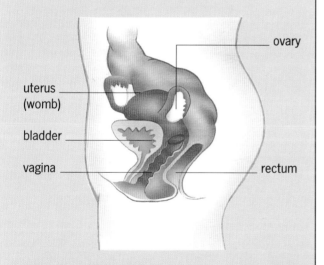

uterus (womb)

bladder

vagina

ovary

rectum

Where do sperm develop?

Sperm are made in the testes – two ovals enclosed in a bag of loose skin that hangs behind the penis. After puberty, a male starts to produce up to 200 million sperm a day. They look like tiny tadpoles. They need the tail to help them swim up the vagina to the egg cell in the Fallopian tube. But first they have a long journey of about 12 in (30 cm) before leaving the man's body. They travel from the testes to a gland beneath the bladder, where they mix with a sticky fluid called semen before being projected down the penis.

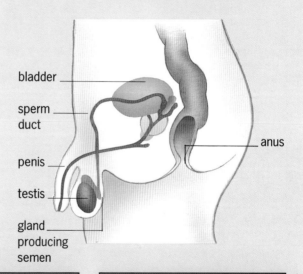

bladder

sperm duct

penis

testis

gland producing semen

anus

DID YOU KNOW...
● A woman's periods stop when she is pregnant and for several months while she is producing milk for the baby?
● Contraception allows a man and woman to have intercourse without the egg cell becoming fertilized?

WHY ARE SOME TWINS IDENTICAL?
Identical twins arise when the fertilized egg splits into two separate parts. Each then develops into a baby. These twins look similar because they started from the same fertilized egg.

DO SPERM LIVE LONG?
Once inside the vagina, sperm have to move fast to reach the egg before they die. They can survive only 1 or 2 days after reaching the womb. Sperm, however, are stored for weeks inside the testicles until needed.

How is the baby formed?

As the fertilized egg moves slowly down the Fallopian tube, the cell divides into two, then into four, and so on. These cells cluster together in a hollow ball. About a week later the ball of cells reaches the womb and sinks itself into the spongy lining of the womb and attaches itself to the womb wall. As the cells go on dividing different kinds of cells appear that will form the placenta and the different parts of the body – the brain and nerves, the heart, liver, bones and so on.

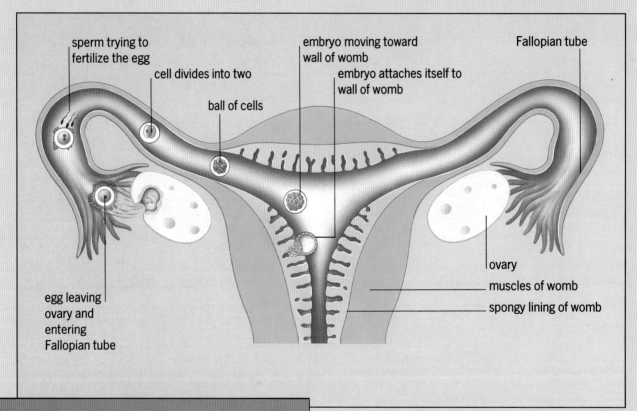

sperm trying to fertilize the egg

cell divides into two

ball of cells

embryo moving toward wall of womb

embryo attaches itself to wall of womb

Fallopian tube

egg leaving ovary and entering Fallopian tube

ovary

muscles of womb

spongy lining of womb

HOW DOES THE EMBRYO DEVELOP?
● After 5 weeks the embryo is about .08 in (2 mm) long. Nervous system is beginning to form.
● After 6 weeks head, chest and stomach have formed. Heart is beginning to form. Arms and legs are just buds. Embryo is about .4 in (1 cm) long.
● After 7 weeks the heart has started to beat.
● After 8 weeks, all the internal organs have formed.
● After 13 weeks, baby is properly formed but its organs are not mature enough to survive if it was born.
● After about 38 weeks, baby has grown to about 20 in (50 cm) and is ready to be born.

What is the placenta?
In the 9 months the baby spends in the womb, it grows from a ball of cells almost too small to see to a fully formed, 7.5-lb (3.4-kg) baby. It gets all the nourishment it needs for this rapid growth from its mother. In the first 13 weeks the placenta forms along with the embryo and attaches itself to the wall of the womb. Food and oxygen are passed from the mother's blood through the placenta to the baby's blood.

What is a fetus?

By the time the embryo is about nine weeks old, it has changed from a ball of cells to a recognizable human shape about 1.2 in (3 cm) long. From now on it is called a fetus. Seven months later it has 2 billion cells and is about 20 in (50 cm) long. Every part of its body has developed, even its nails and hair.

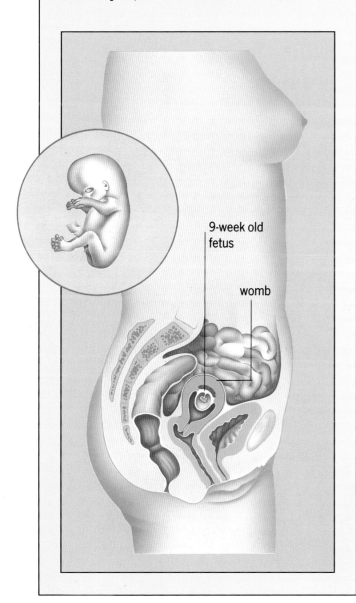

9-week old fetus

womb

How is the baby born?

As the baby grows inside the womb, the walls of the womb stretch and grow with it. After about 38 weeks, the placenta begins to fail and the baby is ready to be born. The neck of the womb stretches and opens. Then the muscular walls of the womb start to contract and push the baby out.

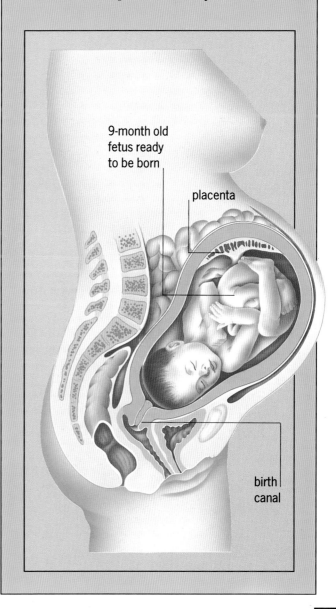

9-month old fetus ready to be born

placenta

birth canal

What makes me a boy or a girl?

Each body cell contains 46 chromosomes that tell the cell what to do. Only the sex cells (sperm and egg cell) contain 23 each. When a sperm and egg join, the new cell then has 46 chromosomes, half from each parent. Two of these chromosomes decide what sex you will be. They are called X and Y. Cells with a Y chromosome become boys.

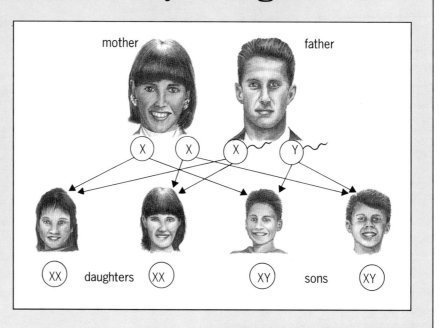

Who do I look like?

You may look more like one parent than the other, but you have inherited characteristics from both. Each chromosome contains hundreds of genes. Genes decide each of your features, like the color of your hair.

WHICH IS DOMINANT?

Some features are decided by just one gene. If you receive two conflicting genes, one of them will be dominant.

● Brown eyes always dominate over blue.

● Free ear-lobes dominate over attached ear-lobes.

● Only the daughter in this family has attached ear-lobes, so both the father and mother must have passed on a hidden, or recessive, gene for attached ear-lobes.

What are hormones?

Hormones are chemical messengers that help to control the body. They are made by various glands and move around the body in your blood. Some act very slowly – those that change you from a child to an adult take several years. Others act rapidly – almost as fast as the nervous system.

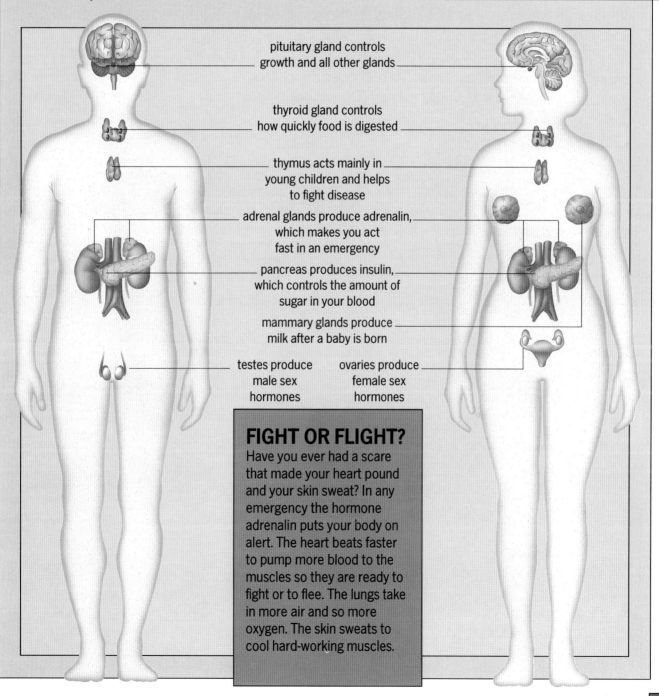

pituitary gland controls growth and all other glands

thyroid gland controls how quickly food is digested

thymus acts mainly in young children and helps to fight disease

adrenal glands produce adrenalin, which makes you act fast in an emergency

pancreas produces insulin, which controls the amount of sugar in your blood

mammary glands produce milk after a baby is born

testes produce male sex hormones

ovaries produce female sex hormones

FIGHT OR FLIGHT?
Have you ever had a scare that made your heart pound and your skin sweat? In any emergency the hormone adrenalin puts your body on alert. The heart beats faster to pump more blood to the muscles so they are ready to fight or to flee. The lungs take in more air and so more oxygen. The skin sweats to cool hard-working muscles.

What is puberty?

Sometime between the ages of 11 and 13 your body will begin to change from that of a child to that of an adult. These changes are called puberty. A girl's hips become broader and her waist narrower. Her voice becomes lower. Breasts begin to develop and periods begin. Boys become more muscular and their voices break and become lower. A boy's penis becomes longer and thicker and hair begins to grow on his face and body.

Both girls and boys grow quickly during puberty. Friendships between boys and girls become important and they begin to feel sexually attracted to each other. Although most people are fully grown by 17, they are still changing emotionally.

HOW CAN I AVOID BEING FAT?

Eating too much sugar and fat will make you overweight and unhealthy. Exercise and the right kind of food will help you to grow strong and look good.
● Eat plenty of fruit, vegetables, cheese, bread and meat, rather than sweets, cakes and fatty foods. A vegetarian diet is healthy but you must eat plenty of protein other than meat.
● Exercise not only makes your muscles stronger, it also increases your stamina so that you do not get tired so quickly. It makes your joints more agile and helps your liver, heart and lungs work better.

WHICH EXERCISE IS BEST?

	Strength	Stamina	Agility	Energy used
Walking to school	*	* *	*	10
Fast walking	*	* * *	*	20
Slow cycling	*	* * *	*	20
Jogging	* *	* * * *	* *	25
Swimming	* * *	* * * *	* * *	35
Fast cycling	* * *	* * * * *	* *	over 40
Disco dancing	*	* * *	* * * *	over 40 (kilojoules/min)

GROWING UP

9 years old

▲ Hamburgers contain protein and carbohydrates. Both are good for you, but you also need fruit and vegetables.

13 years old

17 years old

WHEN WILL I GROW OLD?

Your body starts to age when you are only 30 years old. The cells of the body take longer to renew themselves, so skin becomes wrinkled and muscles weaker. Joints stiffen up and bones become harder. The brain is at its best between 25 and 30, but then begins to slow down. We become old so gradually, most people do not notice until they are over 60 or 70. Old people prefer to do things more slowly. Although they remember the past very well they may forget what happened yesterday. Even so, some 80-year-olds are fitter and more alert than people of 50.

INDEX